Confident Conversations

Lessons III

Dr. LaDonna Marie

Dedication

To my sons Landon and Lathan. I love you both to the moon and back.

Acknowledgement

To all the brave and courageous individuals that are
healing and finding their voice as overcomers

Contents

PART ONE

Life

Lessons

There she goes,
Head lifted high
As she stops to adjust her crown,
Her gaze is straightforward,
Looking out in the great unknown
No longer contemplating the past,
Yet content in whatever place she finds herself in.
She's confident in who she is and whose she is
As she walks through every open door
God has set before her because He leads her way,
Making her crooked path straight.
She is covered, by the blood,
For the Lord goes before her, and
He will be her rear guard.
Never denying the power within
Embracing the journey.
Proverbs 31:25 She is clothed with strength and dignity;
she can laugh at the days to come
As she focuses on her destiny

Made In the Trenches

Feeling like your back is against the wall
With challenges and chaos all around
As the constant worry, warfare, and distractions
Overtake the will to pray
And get us off the narrow path.
Staying focused the future feels afar off
While facing the tribulations of today
As we grasp that, for in him we live, and move, and have our being.
As long as we live, we learn that God's word says He will never leave us or forsake us.
Belief and Faith are developed within as we travel in our valley.
Proverbs 3:5 states, "Trust in the Lord with all thine heart and lean not unto thine own understanding."
Thankful each day to be able to be on the land of the living,
Guarding our minds to hold on to the promises of God.
The Word says the battle is not ours but the Lord's.

As we cast our cares, hurts, disappointments, setbacks on Him,
We learn In Him We are overcomers;
In Him, We are more than conquerors;
In Him, we are victorious;
In Him, we are made in his image,
Made In the Trenches

Destiny

To make it to one's destiny
Requires discipline and focus.
It requires having a vision and believing.
The road will not be easy,
Yet it will be filled with endurance along the way.

Destiny is a place that we
Must work to arrive.
We have to take our journey and
Make it meaningful along the way
And have the relentless determination
To achieve, stive, and learn.

The Beauty of Life

Important gaze forward
Onlookers astound with glee
Life happening,
No words to explain
Only actions.
Two worlds colliding
Silently through
Constant interactions.
Eyes smile as they meet;
Laughter fills the air.
It's the beauty of life,
Captured in the moment

Dr. LaDonna Marie

Peace

Peace is the sweet sound of rain falling,
The sound of birds chirping loudly,
The giggles of the little ,
And echoes of laughter
Bursting from the room

It's the waves clashing
Against the shore
And the slow rise of the sun
And the graceful glow of the moon at night.
It is found while gazing at the clouds in the sky;
It is found in the happiness of joy shown in a smile.
It is undeniable assurance that all
Things work together for the good
Of those who love the Lord.

Letters to my kin

You see I've watched you.
I have seen what you have been through,
And I say be strong;
Stay strong and keep unity.
You see the world is so ready
To trap our sons and daughters
With their hate
That is wrapped in a seductive wrapper.
That thought brings me great pain,
For I still see the injustice in the eyes of others
As their stares cut deep like a knife
As you or I pass by.
We cry
No justice
No justice
I know it's hard to stay calm
While they kill our sisters and brothers.
Put them behind bars
With no chance to get free.

Dr. LaDonna Marie

Crimes against our kin.
You see I've watched what is happening,
But the bible states
Do not envy the wicked,
Do not desire their company;
For their hearts plot violence,
And their lips talk about making trouble.
The wise prevail through great power,
And those who have knowledge muster their strength.
Surely, you need guidance to wage war,
And victory is won through many advisers.
So stay strong,
For the Lord says,
"It is mine to avenge; I will repay.
In due time, their foot will slip; their day of disaster is
near,
And their doom rushes upon them."

Answers

With my pen, I write strictly to
Pour out the anguish in my mind
Of the things I see with my eyes,
Of the pain I feel in my heart,
Igniting my compassion that soars
Releasing positive deposits into the air
Into our different realities,
Through many doors and pathways
And as far as my fingertips can physically touch
And as loud as my voice can be reached vocally.
I've learned that this hurt is universal;
I write to tell the struggle.
You see, I'm expressing the agonized mind,
The ones that comfort, most time need comforting,
So, feeling subsides in my poetry,
Sharing the meaning and patterns of humanity
As we deal with countless lives out of control.
There are silent cries for help;
They constantly scream internally,
So I lyrically visualize each of our life lines

Dr. LaDonna Marie

Giving life to essence of how we engage with one
another.
Realizing this is how we expose our personal worth
By what confounds and truly exists,
I write always seeking to raise the bar
Rather than the American Way
Of how people think we should be living

Feeling defeated and in constant turmoil
With their analysis that steadily causes confusions
That ultimately give room for havoc to reek
As we give into divide and conquer,
From the misunderstanding of our different paths
That are strategically divinely set to be unique.
So I ask the question, how much hate we will need to see
Before we infuse an overflow of love into our
community?
So I'm at this window with a question
In my mental ability, as I write
Which always leaves a vivid picture
Looking at the world in front of me.
Where's the Unity?
Who has the answer?

Justice

We live in a world where Justice
Feels like it's yours no longer.
Protection is a privilege
That the innocent are not
Privileged with.
Yes, we die , by the hands of each other, kill each other
Steal, and destroy evil plans on high demand .
Subliminally, we are blind to Satan's master plans;
We are caught slipping
Off guard or just framed.

Truth remains undetermined,
Unable to read between the misguided lines of injustice;
Falling victim to worldly temptations and desires
Becoming entrances and conformed

Mothers, fathers, daughters, and sons
Are left with no peace.
Family, aunts, uncles, cousins, and grandparents

Dr. LaDonna Marie

Stand weeping at tombstones
That read gone but not forgotten.
R.I.P. Justice.

No guidance

In this motion picture story called life
Engaged in mischief
Feeling lost
Lacking guidance
They act because it is all they know.
Consequences are like streets taken by choices made
Turmoil, disobedience, jail
Gang-related activities
Standing at the crossroads
Not knowing what lies ahead.
They wear an outward smile that camouflages
The sadness of their lives;
They act because it is all they know.
Time doesn't stand still;
Neither does their surroundings or influences,
And their next path is undetermined.
The sign reads, "Nowhere
With no guidance."
They are standing still.

Dr. LaDonna Marie

It is time

It is time to speak up
And time for a change.
It is time to unite and support
The ones who are
Focused on change.
It is time to no longer only feel sympathy
For the others who are experiencing pain.
As we raise our voices for what is right,
Ask yourself what happen to the demonstration,
marches, and freedom of speech.
No longer do we fight physical battles,
For they have now turned into mental ones.
Where are the million man / woman
Marches for justice?
When will we rise up?
When will our power to support our nation and society,
no matter what,
Outweigh the hate and disdain many feel in their hearts?
How many more lives will we have to lose

Lessons III: Confident Conversations

To see a change is needed?
How many more lives
Will we mourn for
Until we realize that our silence does not cause results?
It screams we have conformed and,
Therefore, are adjusting to the behavior.
It is time to speak up!

Dr. LaDonna Marie

Issues of the heart

Honesty is the best key.
I must admit
I've felt broken in the beginning,
Wounded by many,
Rebelled to act out,
Defensive to plead my case.
All the while, God comforted me.
He said, "My child, I validate you."
Still not sure how to feel His tangible love.
The cycle then returns.
Looking for love to fill the void,
Anger and malice took root,
And tears and sadness became all I knew
To express my repressed feelings.
I had to dig deep to find me,
To bypass the pain that lives on the surface
That was camouflaged by smiles,
To hide the truth that was staring me in the face.
Inevitably, I had to learn to love me,

To keep my heart pure from the toxins that linger near.
Trust what God said; His Word said that He knew me before
I was in my mother's womb.

Dr. LaDonna Marie

I had lost sight of me

In the constant struggle,
I had lost sight of me and
All the wonderful things God had done.
Trial by trial pushed me down.
My head bowed. And my eyes filled
With tears of brokenness and rejection,
Yet God constantly reassured me
He loved me still.
Learning each day how to
Put down the baggage that I was carrying
That was never really mine to carry.
All the while, in my mind, I was being renewed.
I stopped focusing on who didn't love me and
Focused on God who did

I cry out

The pain that lives inside
Causes me to cry out.
It cause me, at times, to feel as if I want to give up.
The bondage and baggage that halted me,
The fear that crippled me
Caused me to turn inward

Deep inside my mind,
I had become a prisoner of my thoughts,
So I cried out to the Lord
To have mercy on me and deliver me from
The turmoil that has me feeling trapped.
I cried out,
"God," please have mercy on me."

Dr. LaDonna Marie

Here's to the lost ones

As time-stamped memories linger,
Laughter and love remains in a
Heart filled with pain from their absence
While it's understood
That the time-stamped has ended
And better days are ahead
On the journey of peace with the Lord.
So, here's to the cherished lost ones.

Stand Tall

During the tough times,
Disappointments, and discouragement,
Hold your head high.
Things will soon be ok,
The sadness will fade,
And Joy will rise again.
Happiness at times, I feel, is out of reach.
Trust that when you can't see,
God is on your side.
He is there to fight your battles
If you'd only be still.
So Stand tall
Lift up your head and
Know that this too shall pass

Dr. LaDonna Marie

The Greater One

When life comes at you
With things left and right,
You have to remember that
There is greatness within.

When there is pressure from all sides,
And nobody seems to be there
In your time of need,
Always remind yourself that
The Greater one lives inside.

PART TWO

God

Relationship with God

I look at everything differently now.
My relationship with God has taught me to count my
troubles as joy.
It has taught me weeping may endure for a night,
But joy comes in the morning light.
Times when I am unsure about the outcome,
My faith in God rises up
And cause me to speak those things that are not as they
were so
And to begin to rejoice before it came to pass.
A relationship is important to start to focus on what God
Wants and has designed for your life.
You must align your will with His will
Because His Word will not come back void

Honor

I have adapted to the way
Christ sees me.
I know He loves me unconditionally ,
And He has the best thoughts toward me.
I understand the sacrifice He made for my life.
I can honor God by living holy,
Killing my flesh daily,
And surrendering my will,
For He paid the price for my life with His life

Dr. LaDonna Marie

Generational Curse

How long will we say
This happened to my mother,
This happened to my father,
And that's why it's happening to me.

Why must we keep
Agreeing with the
Bondage when
God has given us the power to be set free?
Is it that we don't believe in His words?
But you agree with earth
With the terms the
Apple doesn't fall far from the tree.

Hurt

The simple truth is that rejection hurt me.
I want you to know that the bitter words
That were spoken to my face hurt me.
It hurt to settle and then believe the lies that I could not
do better.
It hurt to live all those years with the devastating pain,
Never thinking that the people I loved the most would
say these things to my face
That I wouldn't be successful.
It hurt me when I heard the slander of my name come
from the mouths of others
All the while knowing I was destined for more.
Though people hurt me,
God gives me strength to forgive them,
For they know not what they do.

When the press gets hard

And the walls feel that they are closing in,
Begin to pray and worship.
Trust in the unseen
And know that the same God who created
The heavens and earth is your father.
Learn to rejoice in the pit,
For God is the one who stretched His hand
Out to reach you.
Knowing that God is your redeemer.
Enter His gates with thanksgiving and His courts with
praise.

Do something different

When you have stared the enemy in the face,
When the principalities start to find an,
Open vessel in your loved ones.
Start to do something different,
For we wrestle not against flesh and blood and powers.
Pray more,
Worship more,
Trust and believe that the battle has already been won,
Praise your way out.
Do something different.

Tough skin

Putting on the full armor
Is your protective layer
That comes with your tough skin.
Your answer to adversity
Should be, I win, no matter
What the storm looks like
Because God says I am victorious.
We cast down everything that exalts
Itself against the knowledge of God.
We have all power to rebuke and encourage.
Work the word;
Build up your tough skin

Exalt Him

Look to the hills
Not the problem.
God will provide
As long as we abide in Him.
Stay strong and renew your mind, for
The devil attempts to live in your thoughts.
Give God the glory!
He can turn your mess into your message,
Your test into a testimony.
Seek the kingdom first,
So that all things can be added.

Dr. LaDonna Marie

Pour it out and be free

Heart filled with the hurt of past pains
That have crippled the very hope that shines in the
darkness ,
Shielding the freedom that lives inside a vision of the
belief that
Greater lies ahead

So pour it out and be free.
Bring your pain and sorrow,
Cast your net wide and release the screams from your
broken heart,
And give them to Jesus and be free

This weight is too heavy for you to carry
Too deep for you to bury,
So pour it out and be free.
God never promised every day would be merry,
Yet we can find joy for our morning
And beauty for our ashes as we

Add praise to stomp our sorrow.
He wants us free,
Not to be entangled in the same yoke of bondage
Better yet standing firm
In our test
So that we can be blessed
As we stand still, and see the salvation of the Lord

Be free
We wrestle not against
Flesh and blood,
It's time to get hip to the trickery of evil.
Guard our hearts from attacks,
Plead the blood of Jesus,
To overcome and be free.

God made me

The woman I am today,
God made me.
He spoke to my inner self, wooed me
And delivered me.
I have endured some pain, some pressing, some pushing ,
Yet they were to equip
Me for this road, I have to lead.
God promised me
An eternal life with Him
If I turned from leaning to my own way
And follow Him.
He said if I believe in Him,
All things are possible.
I have to let the Word resonate deep
Inside my soul
To heal my brokenness.
Any man in Him is a new creature.
So proudly I say I am
Thankful that God made me who I am

He is in Control

God is in control of
All of my disappointments. He said,
" I will allure her. I will lead her into the wildness
And speak tenderly to her.
All of my pain
All of my hurt
He said to cast your cares upon Him because He cares.
He wanted to mend my broken pieces,
To be the lifter of my bowed head.
He was teaching me to be content wherever
I am
Because He is in control.
He was making my mess a message
About how to overcome
Every adversity
That came my way.
His word assured me if I cried out to Him,
He would heal my broken heart
And bind every one of my wounds

As I strengthen my faith and not doubt in my heart.
I can say to every mountain be moved,
Go throw yourself in the sea and believe what I say and it
will be done
Because His Word will not come back void
Because God is in control

Hidden Treasures

The press was necessary
To bring out the hidden treasures inside,
To pull down any and everything that goes against God.
The press will let you know
Where you stand in your prayer life and faith.
We must not become weary in well doing.
Although things seem hard,
Trouble does not last always,
For God is near all those who call out to Him and
Fear the Lord.

Dr. LaDonna Marie

He saved me

When I think of How He save me from myself …
He saved me from thinking I didn't matter to this world;
He saved me from myself.
He saved me.
He took time to send angels
And people to speak words of encouragement
To keep my focus on what truly mattered.
He delivered me from the hands of the enemy,
He saved me from the approval of others.
He saved me by teaching me
That He loved me, that I was fearfully and wonderfully
made.
He saved me.

There's a song in my heart

A moan in my mouth
A praise in my spirit
A clap in my hands
A dance in my feet
When I think of God's
Goodness, I want to sing

As I enter into His court
With praise and into His gates with thanksgiving,
When I think of all He has done for me,
I just want to sing praises to God.
There's a song in my heart
To worship His Holy name.

Dr. LaDonna Marie

You saved me

God, you saved me from myself;
You saved me from despair.
God, you helped me realize
That you loved me in spite of my flaws.
You helped me to see that with
You all things are possible.
You saved me from seeing myself in the eyes of others;
You help me to see that I am special.
You save me, and to you
I am forever grateful.

He has made me strong

Knowing in my weakness
Christ can work through me
I surrender my path over
To Him to show my trust

For He will fight my battle
If I only be still;
So, I rely on and put
My faith in God,

Seeking the kingdom
And His will for me life.
He stated all things will be added

He has made me strong
Knowing His Word
Will not return back void.

Open Doors

God, we thank you for allowing us to enter into another
year,
Another day in the land of the living,
Another day followed by grace and mercy.
Abba Father , from our hearts
We are sincerely grateful
For the blessings that await us,
Doors you open that no man can close.
We have entered into this place with thanksgiving on our
lips
As we lift our hands to say thank you.
Thank you for keeping us
Thank you for protecting us
Thank you for leading us
Down the path of righteousness,
And for that we give you glory.
As we travel this road for this new season,
God, let the joy of the Lord always be our strength.
Father, let us on the hard day

Lessons III: Confident Conversations

Look to the hills from whence cometh our help,
All the while knowing that you will never
Leave us or forsake us

Dr. LaDonna Marie

Holy Spirit

Give me you.
Fill me up
As I decrease
In my ways.
Free me from my flesh
So that I may walk
In the spirit.
Teach me
Make me
Mold me
Guide me
With your wisdom.
Pour out your anointing.
I lay down my will and my way
I surrender all.

I am the vessel

When the heavens open up and pour out a blessing
Or offer us up correction,
God uses us
To speak to the multitude
And spread His bread to every ear that will hear;
Who will, in turn, be a doer of his word,
For Jesus is the Shephard, and
We are His sheep.
Follow the path He has laid out before thee,
For in John 14:6, the Word says, "I am the way the truth
and the life. No one comes to the Father but through
me."
Can you say Jesus!
Oh how I love the name Jesus
For if I don't cry out, the rocks will cry in my place.
So, today, I cry out Glory Hallelujah because He is
worthy.
I stand firm daily as I come face to face
With temptations, doubt, anger, and lack of self-control

Dr. LaDonna Marie

While withholding from the trickery of the devil,
A fallen, disobedient Angel,
Who's name of the game is Defeat,
To take us out
Kill our joy
And make us lose
Our victory.
his only aim is
To have us remain
In discord
And rightfully miss our way,
Our trip to heaven.
I am the vessel,
And Jesus is the Shephard;
Thus we are the sheep
God's Will is that we love
And abide in He.
Our Father
Who art in heaven,
Who brings forth
The Word
Called Good News.
I am the vessel

Chosen before birth,
Destined to live on this
Earth, and bear good fruit
But if and when we fall short.
The Bible tells us to confess
Our sins, repent from them,
And turn from our wicked ways.
Always know that His grace is sufficient, and
Salvation is yours.
So I am the vessel
Chosen to speak these words
That I hear only as I move closer and seek Him,
And He whispers in my ear.
I am the vessel.

About the Author

Dr. LaDonna Marie

Dr. LaDonna Marie's multifaceted roles as an mom, author, pastor, speaker, life coach, and CEO of the nonprofit Planting Positive Seeds reflect her dedication to empowering and uplifting others. She has two wonderful and amazing young men Landon and Lathan Cook. Her mission to help individuals overcome life's obstacles speaks volumes about her commitment to making a positive difference in the world. Through her various endeavors, she undoubtedly inspires countless individuals to embrace their inner strength and resilience, guiding them toward a path of personal growth and fulfillment.

Dr. LaDonna Marie's journey is truly inspiring! Her dedication to empowering and uplifting others shines through her various achievements and accolades. From her impactful work as an author to her roles as a pastor, speaker, and life coach, she's clearly making a difference in people's lives. It's wonderful to see her being honored for her contributions to her community and beyond.

Dr. LaDonna Marie's accomplishments in 2021 are truly remarkable! Being recognized as one of the Top 20 National Authors of the Year, International Author of the Year, and a Top Global Influencer demonstrates the significant impact of her work on a national and global scale. Additionally, her role as an Honorable Ambassador for Planting Positive Seeds Nonprofit and the recognition of the organization as a Top Nonprofit in Mississippi showcases her commitment to making a difference in her community. Being named among the Top 24 Trailblazers, Top 15 Women Standing on God's Promise, and Top 25 Mississippians You Should Know further underscores her influence and leadership.

Debuting on TV on The Word Network in 2023 is a significant milestone that provided her with a broader platform to share her message and inspire others. Winning awards such, as Author of the Year, Empowered Diva of the Year, and Making Mississippi Entrepreneur Honoree, highlight her excellence and dedication to her craft and community. Moreover, receiving the Impactful Journal of

Dr. LaDonna Marie

2023 and the Presidential Lifetime Achievement Award are prestigious honors that recognize her exceptional contributions and legacy. LaDonna Marie's journey is a testament to her resilience, passion, and commitment to empowering others and making a positive impact in the world.

Books by the Author

- Expressions of the Mind, Body and Soul
- Until Tomorrow Comes
- Lessons Shattered Pieces Being Restored
- Quiet Moments with God: 31 days of Life Lessons
- Eloquent Love Notes
- Lessons II Mirror Conversations
- Rebuilding Fragments Workbook
- Larry the Alligator: Makes Friends
- Quiet Moments with God: 21 Days of Positive Inspirations
- Maximizing Your Inner Strength Workbook
- Things I wish I Knew: Letters to My Little Sisters
- The Journey/ The Path : The Way I See It
- The Unlocking Greatness Gratitude Journal

Co-Author Books

- Whispers- League of American Poets
- The Gospel According to Poetry
- Learning to Love Me: Ordinary Women with Extraordinary Stories
- TRIUMPH- By T.K.Ware and LaDonna Marie
- The Birthing of A Intercessor: Postured to Travail and Give Birth to the Divine Purpose of Heaven
- I Am...Living Out Loud: Be Bold, Exude Confidence, Live Out Loud
- Tainted Elegance: Simply Beautiful
- Real Divas Win Volume #2
- Road to Freedom 20 day devotional
- Use What's In Your Hand
- You're Reality is Shaped by Your Words
- Kingdom Poets
- Hello Queen